KT-493-346

Bromley Libraries

30128 80173 368 7

Canals

Diyan Leake

Raintree is an imprint of Capstone Global Library Limited, a company incorporated in England and Wales having its registered office at 7 Pilgrim Street, London, EC4V 6LB – Registered company number: 6695582

www.raintreepublishers.co.uk
myorders@raintreepublishers.co.uk

Text © Capstone Global Library Limited 2015
First published in 2014
The moral rights of the proprietor have been asserted.

All rights reserved. No part of this publication may be reproduced in any form or by any means (including photocopying or storing it in any medium by electronic means and whether or not transiently or incidentally to some other use of this publication) without the written permission of the copyright owner, except in accordance with the provisions of the Copyright, Designs and Patents Act 1988 or under the terms of a licence issued by the Copyright Licensing Agency, Saffron House, 6–10 Kirby Street, London EC1N 8TS (www.cla.co.uk). Applications for the copyright owner's written permission should be addressed to the publisher.

Edited by Joanna Issa and Penny West
Designed by Philippa Jenkins
Original illustrations © Capstone Global Library Ltd 2014
Picture research by Mica Brancic
Production by Helen McCreath
Originated by Capstone Global Library Ltd
Printed and bound in China

ISBN 978 1 406 28388 4
18 17 16 15 14
10 9 8 7 6 5 4 3 2 1

British Library Cataloguing in Publication Data
Leake, Diyan
      Canals (Water, Water Everywhere!)
A full catalogue record for this book is available from the British Library.

Acknowledgements
We would like to thank the following for permission to reproduce photographs: Alamy pp. 5 (© Robin Weaver), 7 (© LOOK Die Bildagentur der Fotografen GmbH), 10 (© idp canal collection), 11 (© Robert Harding World Imagery), 14 (© Chris Howes/Wild Places Photography), 16, 23c (© Steven May), 17 (© David Reed), 18 (© Barrie Neil), 21 (© Convery flowers), 22b (© Peter Fakler), 22c (© idp canal collection), 23b (© Chris Howes/Wild Places Photography); Getty Images pp. 6 (AFP Photo/Carl de Souza), 12 (National Geographic/Jonathan Kingston), 19 (The Image Bank/Jamie Marshall - Tribaleye Images); Shutterstock pp. 4 (© Leonid Andronov), 9 (© Oleksandr Kalinichenko), 13 (© Chris Jenner), 20 (© David P. Lewis), 22a (© Kevin Eaves), 23a (© Irina Fischer); Superstock p. 15 (JTB Photo).

Cover photograph reproduced with permission of Alamy (© Terry Mathews).
Back cover photograph reproduced with permission of Shutterstock/© Oleksandr Kalinichenko.

We would like to thank Michael Bright and Diana Bentley for their invaluable help in the preparation of this book.

Every effort has been made to contact copyright holders of material reproduced in this book. Any omissions will be rectified in subsequent printings if notice is given to the publisher.

All the Internet addresses (URLs) given in this book were valid at the time of going to press. However, due to the dynamic nature of the Internet, some addresses may have changed, or sites may have changed or ceased to exist since publication. While the author and publisher regret any inconvenience this may cause readers, no responsibility for any such changes can be accepted by either the author or the publisher.

Contents

Canals

Canals are waterways.

Canals are like roads for boats and ships to go on.

People build canals.

Canals look like rivers but they have straight sides.

Canals of the world

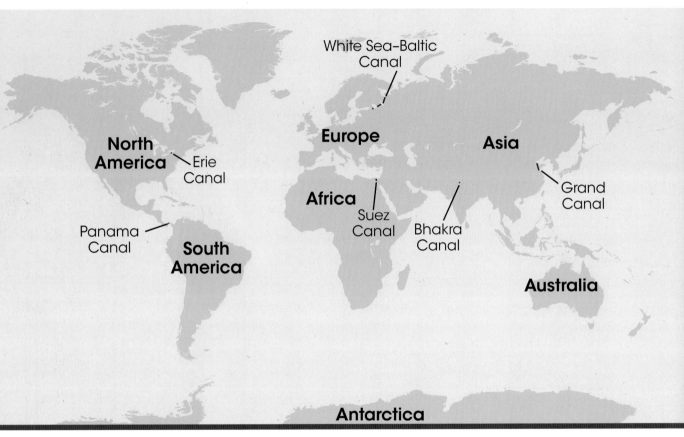

White Sea–Baltic Canal

Europe

Asia

North America

Erie Canal

Africa

Suez Canal

Bhakra Canal

Grand Canal

Panama Canal

South America

Australia

Antarctica

There are canals all over the world.

The Suez Canal is one of the
biggest canals in the world.

Boats and ships on canals

Some canals are small. Boats travel through small canals.

Some canals are big. Ships travel through big canals.

Canals can join one sea
to another.

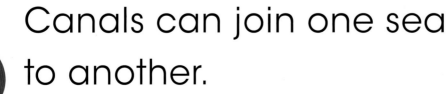
12

Barges carrying cargo go through canals like this.

Where do canals go?

Some canals go through
the countryside.

Some canals go through
towns and cities.

Some canals have locks.

Locks are like steps going up
and down a canal.

Holidays on canals

People go on holiday on canals.

This holiday barge is in the
country of India.

Having fun on canals

It is fun to spend time on a canal.

Stay safe! Always have an adult with you when you are near water.

21

Quiz

Which of these is a canal?

A

B

C

Answer on page 24

Picture glossary

barge flat-bottomed boat used on canals to carry people or goods

countryside land away from towns and cities

lock part of a canal with gates at each end for a boat to pass through

Index

Answer to quiz on page 22: Picture **C** shows a canal.

Note to parents and teachers

Before reading

Ask the children if they have ever visited a canal. Encourage those who have to describe what they did on their visit, and what they saw while they were there. Find out what the children already know about canals. Do they know the difference between a canal and a river? Do they know what people use canals for?

After reading

• Turn to page 10. Explain that these boats are called narrow boats. Ask the children to suggest why the boats are so narrow. Explain that some people live on narrow boats. Display photos of the interior of a narrow boat downloaded from the Internet, or watch a video tour. Discuss what it might be like to live on a narrow boat.

• Show the children examples of canal ware or show them photographs of canal ware downloaded from the Internet. Discuss the features of canal ware art and help the children to paint paper plates in canal ware style.